D1489152

Where There's SMOKE, There's SALMON

Also by Michael Levin

What Every Jew Needs to Know About God
Guide to the Jewish Internet
Journey to Tradition

WHERE THERE'S SMOKE, THERE'S SALMON

The BOOK of JEWISH PROVERBS

ᘓᘓᘓᘓᘓᘓᘓᘓᘓᘓᘓᘓᘓᘓᘓᘓᘓᘓ

MICHAEL LEVIN

FALL RIVER PRESS

© 2001 by Michael Levin

This 2008 edition published by Fall River Press,
by arrangement with Kensington Publishing Corp.

All rights reserved. No part of this publication may be reproduced,
stored in a retrieval system, or transmitted, in any form or by any means,
electronic, mechanical, photocopying, recording, or otherwise,
without prior written permission from the publisher.

Fall River Press
122 Fifth Avenue
New York, NY 10011

ISBN-13: 978-1-4351-0593-5
ISBN-10: 1-4351-0593-1

Printed and bound in the United States of America

1 3 5 7 9 10 8 6 4 2

For Suzanne, with all my love

Contents

Foreword by Jenny Graubart, the Author's Mother

If I'd known my son, Michael Levin, was going to be an author, I would have given him a funnier name. Oh, well. Jewish mothers never seem to get it right.

In fact, when I was asked to write this introduction, I really worried about it. In fact, I dreamt about it all night. In my dreams, I finally solved the problem of what to say. I came up with a brilliant foreword. Unfortunately, I forgot what it was when I woke up.

As for Jewish proverbs, all I remember is what I heard from my *own* Jewish mother. (Yes, even Jewish mothers have Jewish mothers.) As an immigrant, she was very proud of leaving the old stuff behind and being a real American. Only one thing was stronger than that imperative—the fear of the evil eye.

When Michael was three years old (and quite precocious, of course), he was riding on the Fifth Avenue bus with his grandma. As the bus passed the Guggenheim Museum, Michael spelled out all the letters. (Perfectly, I might add.) The man next to

Michael was very impressed, so he asked how old Michael was.

"Three," Michael said.

"Five," his grandmother said at the same moment.

Michael was very surprised that his own grandmother didn't know how old he was. The little lie, Grandma later explained, was to ward off the *ayin hara*, the evil eye. If the evil eye doesn't know how old someone is, it can't take him away. At least that's what our superstition says.

There's probably a Jewish proverb that goes along with that concept, but I don't know what it is.

I am very proud of my son's writing ability. Right from the beginning, I encouraged him to be a man of letters—okay, a small child of letters. When he was a little boy, Michael sat on my lap and learned the alphabet by watching me do the crossword puzzle. He learned all the letters, but unfortunately he didn't learn them in the right order.

Well, my son has done a good thing by writing all these books. Anyone can write a sad story and make people cry. But to write things that make people laugh—well, that makes a Jewish mother proud. I hope you enjoy my son's book.

Introduction

The rabbis say that Torah has seventy faces, but psychologists might say that Judaism has multiple personalities. Judaism is perhaps the most paradoxical of all the world's faiths. Its central beliefs have not changed in thousands of years, yet it permits the most questioning. No religion is better known for its sense of humor—or for its sense of tragedy. Traditional forms of Judaism are among the most demanding of all the world's religions; newer forms, among the least. We are the People of the Book—and yet most Jews haven't gone anywhere near a Bible in years. Do Christians and Moslems spend as much time trying to figure out who belongs to their religions? Jews have spent decades—probably even centuries—just trying to figure out who is a Jew.

The broad, three thousand year sweep of Jewish history, therefore, offers a massively rich field of sources from which to draw. We have kabbalists and comedians, victors and victims, Psalmists and sinners, biblical scholars and blasphemers, prophets and professors. And we are drawn, perhaps like no other people on earth, to the written word—to record our every thought, be it spiritual, sinful, or somewhere in between. We Jews today live in a time of amazing contradiction. On the one hand, we have never been so free to practice our faith. On the other hand, we have never felt so distant from it. Beyond the life cycle events—birth, bar and bat mitzvah, marriage, and death—countless Jews today feel alienated from their religion.

The purpose of this book is twofold. First, we will explore the amusing—often wickedly funny—side of Judaism. Second, and at least as important, by offering insights from every time period in Judaism, from the Bible through the Middle Ages to the present day, we hope to give readers a sense of the surprising wisdom, relevance, and depth of Judaism and Jewish literature.

Jews affirm life because, for thousands of years, Judaism has affirmed life, sometimes in unbelievably trying circumstances. How Jews survived, and what we learned along the way, awaits you in these pages.

Special thanks to my phenomenal researcher, Corey Nickerson, for all of her hard work and dedication, and thanks and praise to my fantastic typist, Howard Zilbert, for his excellent work and friendship. High praise to Kenneth J. Silver, who oversaw the production of this book. And finally, a big thank you to my editor, Gary Goldstein, for his friendship, trust, and solid commitment to getting me paid.

From the moment I picked this book up until the moment I put it down, I could not stop laughing. Some day I hope to read it.
GROUCHO MARX

The wise make proverbs and fools repeat them.
ISAAC D'ISRAELI

WHERE THERE'S
SMOKE,
THERE'S
SALMON

1
ADVICE

Never take a front row seat at a bris.

RABBI BENJAMIN SINCOFF, OCEAN PARKWAY
JEWISH CENTER

Be not sweet lest you be swallowed.

MIVCHAR HAPENINIM

One must never stand in a place of
danger expecting a miracle to
protect the faithful.

TALMUD, KIDDUSHIN 39B

Do not hate your brother in your heart.

MOSES, LEVITICUS 19:17

One should not be addicted to jesting and mockery, nor should one be sad and mournful, but cheerful.

MAIMONIDES, *MISHNAH TORAH*

An individual ought to forgive transgressions and to pardon anyone who injures him, whether through speech or deed.

ABRAHAM GALANTE, SIXTEENTH-CENTURY RABBI, SFED, ISRAEL

No one person should walk behind two donkeys.

OLD HUNGARIAN-JEWISH PROVERB

Laugh now, but one day you, too, will be driving a big Cadillac and eating dinner at four in the afternoon.

MR. MORRIS BENDER, CENTURY VILLAGE, PEMBROKE PINES, FLORIDA

One should always assume the habit of silence, and speak only on subjects of wisdom or on matters of vital importance to one's being.

MAIMONIDES, *MISHNAH TORAH*

Do not oppress a stranger—for you know the heart of a stranger, seeing that you were strangers in the land of Israel.

MOSES, EXODUS 23:9

If you're going to whisper at the movies, make sure it's loud enough for everyone to hear.

OVERHEARD AT THE SKYLARK MOVIE THEATER, MIAMI

I am very careful in the choice of enemies.

AHAD HA AM, RUSSIAN JEWISH ZIONIST

When you cast your bread on the water, you get bread and water.

AUTHOR UNKNOWN

Rabbi Ishmael said: Be submissive to a superior, affable to a suppliant, and receive all men with cheerfulness.

TALMUD, AVOT 3:16

Woe to the wicked and woe to his
neighbor.

RASHI, COMMENTARY ON EXODUS

Make your books your companions.
Let your cases and shelves be your
pleasure grounds and orchids. Bask
in their paradise, gather their fruit,
pluck their roses, take their spices.

JUDAH IBN TIBBON, NINETEENTH-CENTURY
AUTHOR

The world is but a narrow bridge and
the main thing is not to fear.

RAV NACHMAN OF BRATISLAVA

Death and life are in the power of
the tongue.

PROVERBS 18:21

Do not envy evil men; do not desire to be with them; for their hearts talk violence and their lips speak mischief.

PROVERBS 24:1–2

Love thy neighbor as thyself—"It lies upon you to love your comrade as one like yourself. And who knows as you do your many defects? As you are nonetheless able to love yourself, so love your fellow, no matter how many defects you may see in him."

BAAL SHEM TOV

Be not like a bird that sees the grain but not the trap.

IBN TIBBON

Approach a goat from the back, a
horse from the front, and a stupid
man from no direction whatsoever.

HUNGARIAN-JEWISH PROVERB

Do not boast of tomorrow, for you
do not know what the day will bring.

PROVERBS 27:1

Do not worry yourself with the
troubles of tomorrow. Perhaps you
will have no tomorrow, and why
should you trouble yourself about a
world that is not yours?

AUTHOR UNKNOWN

When one spits upwards it falls
down on his own face.

MIDRASH, KOHELET RABBAH 7

One should not say with his mouth what he does not mean with his heart.

TALMUD, BABL METZIA

Do not throw stones into a well that once gave you its water.

MIDRASH, TANCHUMA MATTOT 3

The secret of happiness is to forget about yourself.

AUTHOR UNKNOWN

We must keep alive the sense of wonder through *deeds* of wonder.

ABRAHAM JOSHUA HESCHEL, TWENTIETH-CENTURY THEOLOGIAN

In a place where there are no men,
strive to be a man.

TALMUD, AVOT 2:6

He who guards his mouth and
tongue guards himself from evil.

PROVERBS 21:23

To answer a man before hearing him
out is foolish and disgraceful.

PROVERBS 18:13

He who cannot control his temper is
defective in intellect.

IBN GABIROLT

2
ANGER

By three things can a man be known: By his purse, by his drinking cup, and by his temper, and some say, even by his laughter.

RUSSIAN-JEWISH PROVERB

A gentle response allays wrath; a harsh word provokes anger.

PROVERBS 15:1

The sins of the angry man will surely outweigh his merits.

RABBI NACHMAN OF BRATISLAVA

The angry man fills his mouth with live coals and with needles, sharp and hard.

RABBI WOLF ZITOMIRER

If one is hot-tempered, he is told to train himself to the point that even if he is assaulted or insulted, he should pay no attention.

MAIMONIDES, *MISHNAH TORAH*

Don't let your spirit be quickly vexed, for vexation abides in the breasts of fools.

ECCLESIASTES 7:9

Refrain from anger, and you will not sin; drink not to excess, and you will not sin—The Prophet Elijah

TALMUD, BERACHOT 29B (ATTRIBUTED TO THE PROPHET ELIJAH)

3
CHARACTER

It's important to feel guilty.
Otherwise you're capable of terrible
things. Of course, I feel guilty all the
time and I never did anything.
WOODY ALLEN

Half a pair of scissors is a single
scis.
ALAN SHERMAN

Any leader who can't see a distance
of five hundred miles is no leader.
THE STOLINER REBBE

It is easier to fight for principles than to live up to them.

ALFRED ADLER, AUSTRIAN-JEWISH
PSYCHOLOGIST

They will let you live only when you learn to die.

THEODOR HERZL, AUSTRIAN-JEWISH JOURNALIST
AND FOUNDER OF POLITICAL ZIONISM

A man who strays from the path of prudence will rest in the company of ghosts.

PROVERBS 21:16

Rabbi Levitas of Yavnah said: "Be exceedingly lowly of spirit, for the hope of man is but the worm."

TALMUD, AVOT, 4:4

A rabbi whose community does not disagree with him is not really a rabbi. And a rabbi who fears his community is not really a man.

RABBI ISRAEL SALANTER, FOUNDER OF THE MUSSAR (SELF-AWARENESS) MOVEMENT

There's hope, but not for us.

FRANZ KAFKA

There are four types of men: one who says what's mine is mine and what's yours is yours—he is a neutral person. One who says what's mine is yours and what's yours is mine is a fool. One who says what's mine is yours and what's yours is yours is righteous. One who says what's yours is mine and what's mine is mine is evil.

TALMUD, AVOT 5:13

The man who never made an enemy
never made anything.

PAUL MUNI

Three things weaken men's strength:
Fear, travel, and sin.

TALMUD, GITTIN 70A

Jealousy is cruel as the grave; the
calls thereof are calls of fire.

SONG OF SONGS 8:6

The righteous are called living even
when they are dead, and the wicked
are called dead even when they are
living.

AUTHOR UNKNOWN

In accordance with your friends, I measure your wealth. In accordance with your enemies, I measure your greatness.

RABBI LAZEROV

When arrogance appears, disgrace follows.

PROVERBS 11:2

He who loves pleasure comes to want; he who loves wine and oil does not grow rich.

PROVERBS 21:17

The wicked flee though no one gives chase, but the righteous are as confident as lions.

PROVERBS 28:1

He who digs a pit will fall in it, and whoever rolls a stone, it will roll back on him.

PROVERBS 26:27

Charm is deceitful, and beauty is vain, but a woman who fears the Lord is to be praised.

PROVERBS 31:30

Arrogance is a kingdom without a crown.

AUTHOR UNKNOWN

He who asks more of a friend than he can bestow, deserves to be refused.

AUTHOR UNKNOWN

Rabbi Eliezer, the son of Jacob, said:
He who does one good deed has
gotten himself one advocate; and he
who commits one sin has gotten
himself one accuser. Repentance
and deeds of charity are as a shield
against punishment.

TALMUD, AVOT, 4:13

Pray for the welfare of the
government, since, but for the fear
of the government, men would
swallow each other alive.

RABBI CHANINA, TALMUD, AVOT, 3:2

The law is an answer to him who
knows that life is a problem.

RABBI ABRAHAM JOSHUA HESCHEL

Everyone must have two pockets so that he can reach into the one or the other, according to his needs. In his right pocket are to be the words: "For my sake was the world created," and in his left: "I am dust and ashes."

AUTHOR UNKNOWN

Our slavery is that we choose to be slaves.

MALALOT HA TORAH, R, 1828

Hillel used to say, If I'm not for myself, who will be for me? And if I am only for myself, what am I? And if not now, when?

TALMUD, AVUT

It is forbidden to buy from a thief
anything that he has stolen; it is a
grave sin, since one encourages
criminals, thereby inducing a thief to
commit other thefts. If he finds no
customer, he will not steal. "The
partner of a thief is his own enemy."

MAIMONIDES, *MISHNAH TORAH*

He who is compassionate to the
cruel will come, in the end, to be
cruel to the compassionate.

MIDRASH, YALKUT SAMUEL 121

We say to the bee, we want neither
thy honey nor thy sting.

AUTHOR UNKNOWN

A twisted thing cannot be made straight.

ECCLESIASTES 1:15

Do not hate your brother in your heart. You must admonish your neighbor and not bear sin because of him.

LEVITICUS, 19:17

The function of fear is scrupulous observance of the law.

CHAZON ISH

Hath not a Jew eyes? Hath not a Jew hands, organs, dimensions, senses, affections, passions? Fed with the same food, hurt with the same weapons, subject to the same diseases, healed by the same means, warmed and cooled by the same winter and summer, as a Christian is? If you prick us, do we not bleed? If you tickle us, do we not laugh? If you poison us, do we not die? And if you wrong us, shall we not revenge?

WILLIAM SHAKESPEARE, *THE MERCHANT OF VENICE*

4
EAT, DRINK...

According to Jewish dietary law, pork and shellfish may be eaten only in Chinese restaurants.

MOLLY PICON

Ecstasy is what happens between the scotch and soda and the bagels and lox.

SOPHIE TUCKER

A bad matzo ball makes a good paperweight.

WOLFIE COHEN

Never leave a restaurant empty-handed.

WOLFIE COHEN, WOLFIE'S RESTAURANT, MIAMI BEACH

Why is it called a kugel (noodle pudding)? It's shaped like a kugel; it's sweet like a kugel; it's thick like a kugel, and it tastes like a kugel. So why shouldn't we call it a kugel?

MRS. IDA KAMINSKY, FOREST HILLS, NY

To what do I attribute my longevity? Cool mountain water. That and a stuffed cabbage.

MEL BROOKS, AS THE 2000-YEAR-OLD MAN

So what's wrong with a dry turkey?

AUTHOR UNKNOWN

What is a bagel? A bagel is a
doughnut dipped in cement.

YONAH SHIMMEL, YONAH SHIMMEL'S KNISHES,
HOUSTON ST., NEW YORK

Don't let the lox get in your socks,
don't let the soup get in your snoot!

MICKEY KATZ, BORSCHT BELT ENTERTAINER

A schlemiel is a person who always
spills his soup. A schlemozzle is the
person he spills it on.

AUTHOR UNKNOWN

When you are at war and lay seige to
a city . . . do not destroy its trees by
taking the ax to them, for they
provide you with food.

DEUTERONOMY 20:19

A sated person disdains honey, but to a hungry man anything bitter seems sweet.

PROVERBS 27:7

The only revenge I would take on the captured Egyptian soldiers would be to make them eat the same food *our* boys eat.

MOSHE DAYAN, AFTER THE 1967 SIX-DAY WAR

Do not eyeball that red wine as it lends its color to the cup, as it flows on smoothly; in the end, it bites like a snake; it spits like a basilisk. Your eyes will see strange sights, your heart will speak distorted things.

PROVERBS 23:31–33

Do not eat of a stingy man's food;
do not crave for his dainties. He is
like one keeping accounts; "Eat and
drink," he says to you, but he does
not really mean it.

PROVERBS 23:6–7

Sugar in the mouth won't help if
you're bitter in the heart.

YIDDISH PROVERB

As long as a person takes plenty of
exercise, does not overeat, and
keeps his bowels regulated, he will
contract no illness, even though he
eats inferior food.

MAIMONIDES, *MISHNAH TORAH*

Drink water from your own well.

PROVERBS 5

A person who swallows a wasp
cannot live.

TALMUD, GITTIN 70A

Spend less than you can afford on
food, as much as you can afford on
clothes, and more than you can
afford on your wife and children.

MAIMONIDES, *MISHNAH TORAH*

If you eat your bagel, you'll have
nothing in your pocket but the hole.

AUTHOR UNKNOWN

Rabbi Zwi Chaim Yisroel, an orthodox scholar of the Torah and the man who developed whining to an art unheard of in the West, was unanimously hailed as the wisest man of the Renaissance by his fellow-Hebrews, who totaled a sixteenth of one percent of the population. Once, when he was on his way to synagogue to celebrate the sacred Jewish holiday commemorating God's reneging on every promise, a woman stopped him and asked the following question: "Rabbi, why are we not allowed to eat pork?"

"We're not?" the Rabbi said incredulously. "Uh-oh."

WOODY ALLEN, *GETTING EVEN*

Do not make a stingy sandwich;
pile the cold cuts high.
customers should see salami
coming through the rye.

ALAN SHERMAN

"Where there's smoke, there's
salmon."

BARNEY GREENGRASS, OWNER OF A LEGENDARY
UPPER WEST SIDE FISH STORE

"When I was a kid, my mother
always said, 'Clean your plate—
children are starving in Europe.'
Years later I went to Europe and
what did I see? A bunch of fat
schlubs."

BILLY CRYSTAL

There is nothing worthwhile for a
man but to eat and drink and afford
himself enjoyment within his means.

ECCLESIASTES 3:24

Better a dry crust of bread with
peace than a house full of feasting
with spite.

PROVERBS 17:1

Who cries woe, alas; who has
quarrels; who complains; who has
wounds without cause; who has
bleary eyes? Those whose wine
keeps till the small hours, those who
gather to drain the cups.

PROVERBS 29:30

Hunger dominates the world when justice is not tempered with mercy.
THE ZOHAR

The two things Jews know best are suffering and where to find good Chinese food.
NORMAN STEINBERG, FROM *MY FAVORITE YEAR*

5
FAMILY

Without Jewish mothers, who would
need therapy?

BEATRICE KAUFMAN (MRS. GEORGE S.
KAUFMAN, THE GREAT JEWISH PLAYWRIGHT)

If a father does not teach his son a
trade, it is as if he taught him to be
a thief.

TALMUD, KIDDUSHIN 28

The world is only maintained by the
breath of schoolchildren.

MAIMONIDES, *MISHNAH TORAH*

A stupid son is a calamity to his
father; the nagging of a wife is like
the endless dripping of water.

PROVERBS 19:13

My parents were very poor. They
couldn't afford to buy me a pet dog.
So they bought me an ant. They told
me it was a dog. I was a dumb kid,
what did I know? I named him Spot.

WOODY ALLEN

And God will turn the hearts of the
parents to the children, and the
hearts of the children to their
parents.

MALACHI 3:24

The father of the husband and the father of the wife are no more kinsmen than is a basket to a barrel.

TALMUD, SANHEDRIN 28B

Do not withhold discipline from a child; if you beat him with a rod he will not die. Beat him with a rod and you will save him from the grave.

PROVERBS 24:14

Honor thy father and mother, that thy days may be long upon the land which the Lord they God gives to you.

EXODUS 20:12

When the parent helps the child,
they both laugh. When the child
helps the parent, they both cry.

AUTHOR UNKNOWN

"I thank God for my sons," said an
elderly man. "My firstborn is a
doctor. The second is a lawyer; the
third, a chemist; the fourth, an artist;
and the fifth, a writer."

"What do you do?" he was asked.

"I," said the man, "have a dry
goods store. Not a very big one, but
I manage to support them all."

AUTHOR UNKNOWN

"What do you mean, he'll have two
mothers? Most people barely survive
one!"

WOODY ALLEN TO MERYL STREEP IN
MANHATTAN

6
FAITH

There is no Judaism without love
and fear, wonder and awe, faith and
concern, knowledge and
understanding.

ABRAHAM JOSHUA HESCHEL

The greatest redefiner of Jewish
identity has been Hitler.

ISAAC DEUTSCHER, HISTORIAN

Man makes religion, religion does
not make man.

KARL MARX

Is it not easier for a camel to descend through the eye of a needle than to find a rent-controlled, two-bedroom apartment in New York City?

SOL WEINSTEIN & HOWARD ALBRECHT, AUTHORS OF *LOXFINGER* and other spoofs

It suddenly occurred to me that there's a very simple meaning in talking about oneself as a Chosen People: if you are chosen, *you cannot choose.* The Jews are a Chosen People because they have no choice.

LESLIE FIEDLER, AUTHOR

Jews are the Chosen People—chosen for tsuris!

MRS. IDA PINCUS OF BROOKLYN (AND TWO WEEKS EVERY WINTER IN MIAMI BEACH)

Anti-Semitism . . . is the swollen
envy of pygmy minds—meanness,
injustice.

MARK TWAIN

If one keeps but one Sabbath
properly, it is regarded as if he had
observed all the Sabbaths from the
day on which God created His world
to the time of the resurrection of the
dead.

MECHILTA, EXODUS 31:16

How I would love to cuddle with the
Sabbath queen.

JULIUS LESTER, AN AFRICAN-AMERICAN 1960s
REVOLUTIONARY WHO CONVERTED TO JUDAISM

I give you these fifteen . . . (drops a tablet) . . . I give you these ten commandments!

MEL BROOKS, *HISTORY OF THE WORLD, PART I*

It is part of man's condition that he must endure time and change: seas, rivers, deeps, deserts, and wildernesses filled with serpents and scorpions. Only thus can he be worthy of entering the gates of holiness.

RABBI NACHMAN OF BRATISLAVA

Even when the gates of heaven are closed to prayer, they are open to tears.

RABBI ELEAZAR-BE PADAT, A LEADING THIRD-CENTURY TALMUDIC SCHOLAR

The gravest sin for a Jew is to forget
what he represents.

ABRAHAM JOSHUA HESCHEL

The Sabbath is a reminder of the
two worlds—this world and the world
to come; it is an example of both
worlds. For the Sabbath is joy,
holiness, and rest; joy is part of this
world; holiness and rest are
something of the world to come.

MENORAT HA-MAOR (*Candelabra of Light*)

What was created on the seventh
day? Tranquility, serenity, peace,
and repose.

GENESIS, RABBAH 10:9

I keep trying to think, but nothing happens!

CURLY HOWARD (HORWITZ), ONE OF THE THREE STOOGES

Stand by your mensch.

TAMMY WYNETSKY

To pray is to know how to stand still and to dwell upon a word.

ABRAHAM JOSHUA HESCHEL

On Yom Kippur, instead of striking your heart at the mention of every sin, your heart should strike you.

CHOFETZ CHAIM, THEOLOGIAN

Go your way, eat your bread with joy and drink your wine with a merry heart, for God has already accepted your works.

MIDRASH (THE HEAVENLY VOICE THAT SPEAKS AT THE END OF YOM KIPPUR)

Sin crouches at the doorway.

GENESIS

Religion consists of God's question and man's answer.

ABRAHAM JOSHUA HESCHEL

I will restore to you the years that the locust has eaten.

THE PROPHET JOEL

Selfishness is the only real atheism.
ISRAEL ZANGWILL, NOVELIST

How goodly are your talents,
O Jacob; your dwelling places,
O Israel!
NUMBERS 24:5

It is not the Jews who have kept the
Sabbath—it is the Sabbath that has
kept the Jews.
ANCIENT PROVERB

Israel falls but rises to stand once
more.
YALKUT NITZABIN 940

Art is a form of prayer.
FRANZ KAFKA

A true dream originates through an angel, while a false one originates through a demon.

TALMUD, BERACHOT 55B

A man is forbidden to wear even a single garment worn by women, even though he would be recognized as a man by the rest of his garments. A woman is likewise forbidden to wear even a single garment worn by men. This includes ornaments and articles like cosmetics.

JOSEPH CARO, SIXTEENTH-CENTURY ORTHODOX RABBI

It is impossible to have a dream that does not contain worthless information.

TALMUD, BERACHOT 55B

In a dream, in a vision of the night . . .
God opens the ears of man.

JOB 33:15–16

What poetry there is in human tears.

HEINRICH HEINE, NINETEENTH-CENTURY GERMAN-JEWISH POET

The wave of a song carries the soul
to heights which utterable meanings
can never reach.

ABRAHAM JOSHUA HESCHEL

There are halls in heaven that open
only to the voice of song.

THE ZOHAR

Why are four questions asked on Passover and no questions on Yom Kippur or Rosh Hashanah? Because to see a Jew upset and moan is not unusual and raises no questions, but to see a Jew happy—that demands an explanation.

CANTOR MORRIS DUBINSKY, NEW YORK CITY

7
GOD

God is higher than time.

RAV NACHMAN OF BRATISLAVA

And God saw everything which he had made, and behold, it was very good.

GENESIS 1:31

God does not play dice with the universe.

ALBERT EINSTEIN

Woe to those who get up at dawn to
chase after liquor, who tarry into
evening while wine inflames them . . .
The deeds of God they do not
regard, and the work of his hands
they do not see.

ISAIAH 5:11–12

It has been told you, O man, what is
good, and what the Lord requires of
you: only to do justly, and to love
mercy, and to walk humbly with
God.

MICAH 6:8

If you kept account of sins, O Lord,
who would survive?

PSALM 130:4

The rabbis of the Talmud say that
"very good" refers to the evil
impulse for "were it not for that
impulse, a man would not build a
house, marry a wife, beget children,
or conduct business affairs."

MIDRASH, GENESIS RABBAH 9:7

The slave is the same child of God
that I am.

RABBI YOHANAN (199–279), THE COMPILER
OF THE JERUSALEM TALMUD

When a Nazi guard asked a Jewish
Holocaust inmate why he prayed
every day, the Jew replied, "I thank
God every day that He did not make
me like you."

FROM A VIDEO SHOWN AT THE END OF ONE'S
VISIT TO THE HOLOCAUST MUSEUM,
WASHINGTON, DC

One who deceives his fellow man
deceives his Maker.

TALMUD, *KALLAH* 10

Schlag dich mit Gott herum. (Go
fight God.)

AUTHOR UNKNOWN

We pray that God may accept our
call for help. But we also pray that
God, who knows that which is
hidden, may hear the silent cries of
our souls.

RABBI URI OF STRELISK

I hope I can love a *tsaddik* (a
righteous person) as much as God
loves a wicked man.

BAAL SHEM TOV

A thief, while breaking into a home in order to steal, calls upon God to help him.

RABBI SHNEUR ZALMAN OF LIADI, FOUNDER OF THE CHABAD MOVEMENT

God's gift of the power of speech was as important as the creation of the world.

RABBI HAMA BEN HANINA, THIRD-CENTURY TALMUDIC SCHOLAR

Just as the Lord feels pity for man, he has pity for animals.

MIDRASH, DEVARIM RABBAH 6:1

Rely on God with all your heart and trust not your own understanding.

PROVERBS 3:5

We pray that God may accept our call for help. But we also pray that God, who knows that which is hidden, may hear the silent cries of our souls.

RABBI URI OF STRELISK

Unless the Lord builds the house, they labor in vain who build it; unless the Lord guards the city, the watchmen awaken in vain.

PSALMS 127:1

God is of no importance unless he is of supreme importance.

ABRAHAM JOSHUA HESHCEL

Whatever.

BAMBI SHAPIRO, AGE 16, SHERMAN OAKS, CALIFORNIA

When speaking with others, or
attending to our bodily wants, our
mind is all the time with God; and
we are with our heart constantly
near God.

MAIMONIDES, *THE GUIDE FOR THE PERPLEXED*

The Lord is my shepherd; I shall not
want.

PSALMS 23:1

God says: A son honors his father
and a servant his master. If I then
am a father, where is the honor due
Me? And if I am a master, where is
the respect due Me?

MALACHI 1:6

As one thinks of God in his heart, so
does God think of him.

THE RAV OF MEDZIBEZH

Wherever a Jew goes, his God goes with him.

RABBI TANHUMA BAR ABBA, FOURTH-CENTURY TALMUDIC SCHOLAR

True worship is not a petition to God. It is a sermon to ourselves.

EMIL G. HIRSCH, GERMAN-JEWISH INDUSTRIALIST

And all your children shall be taught of the Lord, and great shall be the peace of your children.

ISAIAH 54:13

Do God's will as if it were your will, that He may do your will as if it were His will.

TALMUD, AVOT 2:4

Nothing is more dear to the Lord
than modesty.

AUTHOR UNKNOWN

We pray that God may accept our
call for help. But we also pray that
God, who knows that which is
hidden, may hear the silent cries of
our souls.

RABBI URI OF STRELISK

Where were you when I laid the
earth's foundation? Tell, if you
know so much. Who sits in
measurements? Surely you know!
Or who stretched the line out on it?

JOB 38:4–5

God is a tear that human beings
weep over their own destiny.

LUDWIG FERBACH

Rabbi Judah, in the name of Rav,
explains how God spends his day: In
the first three hours, God sits and
occupies Himself with the Torah. In
the next three, He sits and judges
the whole world; and whenever he
sees that the whole world is guilty,
He rises from His throne of justice,
and sits on the throne of mercy. In
the next three, he sits and feeds the
whole world, from the horned
buffalo to the eggs of the louse. In
the last three, He sits and sports
with leviathan (the great whale), as it
says, leviathan whom you have
made to sport with.

TALMUD, AVODAH ZARAH

Naturally, God will forgive me. That's his business.

HEINRICH HEINE'S FAMOUS LAST WORDS

Rabbi Azariah, in the name of Rabbi Yehudah ben Shimon, said: When the Israelites do God's will, they add to the power of God on high. When the Israelites do not do God's will, they, as it were, weaken the great power of God on high.

MIDRASH, *LAMENTATIONS RABBAH*

A man's fears become a trap for him, but he who trusts in the Lord shall be safeguarded.

PROVERBS 29:25

Neither by armies nor by might but only by my spirit will Israel succeed, says the Lord of Hosts.

ZACHARIAH 4:6

God is not wicked. The worst thing you can say is that He's an underachiever.

WOODY ALLEN

Even God prays. What is his prayer? "May it be My will that My love of compassion overwhelms My demand for strict justice."

TALMUD, BARACHOT 7A

It is not in our power to explain either the prosperity of the wicked or the afflictions of the righteous.

RABBI YANNAI, TALMUDIC SAGE

Rabbi Tanhuma said: "Israel's only happiness consists in the fact that they choose the Holy One, Blessed be He to be their God, and the Holy One, Blessed be He, chooses them to be His special treasure."

MIDRASH, NUMBERS RABBAH

I will send you the prophet Elijah before the great and terrible day of the Lord comes. He will reconcile fathers to sons, and sons to fathers.

MALACHI 4:5

Hear them not, for I am with thee. Be not dismayed, for I am thy God; I strengthen thee, yea, I help thee.

ISAIAH

8
JEWISH HUMOR

The only honest art form is laughter,
comedy. You can't fake it.

LENNY BRUCE

(During the 1930s) A dentist tells a
Jew in Germany, don't be afraid,
and open your mouth. The Jew
responds, "Either one or the other."

AUTHOR UNKNOWN

The girl who stoops to conquer
usually wears a low-cut dress.

HENNY YOUNGMAN

A Jew entered an elegant restaurant and the waiter said, "We don't serve Jews here." "That's okay," said the Jew. "I don't eat Jews."

AUTHOR UNKNOWN

The only thing more important than a good education is a good parking space at the mall.

OVERHEARD IN BOCA RATON, FLORIDA

Jews prove their optimistic nature by cutting a quarter inch off the penis before they even know how long it's going to be.

JACKIE MASON

In a bar, an Irishman noticed a Jew crossing himself every time he took a drink, which was an extremely frequent occurrence. When the Irishman asked why, the Jew explained, "It's a matter of principle with me. Why should I give some anti-Semite a chance to see a Jew drink like a fish?"

AUTHOR UNKNOWN

Can we actually "know" the universe? My God, it's hard enough finding your way around in Chinatown.

MR. SOL MELNICK, MINEOLA, LONG ISLAND

Religion is just insurance in this world against a fire in the next.

AUTHOR UNKNOWN

Two friends go to eat in a restaurant they've never tried before. At the end of the meal, one turns to the other and says, "The food here is terrible." The other replies, "And such small portions."

AUTHOR UNKNOWN

Israel is the greatest place in the world for people, especially for a millionaire. Why? Because no millionaire has died there yet.

JOEY ADAMS

And so the woman said to the beggar, "You have two good arms; why should I give you a penny?" And the beggar replied, "For your lousy penny I should cut off an arm?"

AUTHOR UNKNOWN

They say that KGB headquarters is the tallest building in Moscow, because even though it's only eight stories high, a Jew can see Siberia from the basement.

SOURCE UNKNOWN

Marriage is a three-ring circus: engagement ring, wedding ring, and suffering.

AUTHOR UNKNOWN

My doctor told me to quit smoking cigars. I didn't listen to him. So what happened? The doctor died.

GEORGE BURNS

Insanity is hereditary—you can get it from your children.

GROUCHO MARX

Three Jews are sentenced to death. They are put in front of a firing squad. The officer turns to the first condemned man. "Do you want a blindfold?"

"Yes, sir."

He asks the second one the same question.

"Yes, sir."

He asks the third.

"No, I don't want anything from you."

The second man turns to the third and says to him in a worried voice, "Moishe, don't make trouble now."

AUTHOR UNKNOWN

When a Jew doesn't care for something, he says "It's not my glass of tea."

MEL BROOKS

A lousy businessman is one who goes bankrupt twice and doesn't make a cent either time.

MYRON COHEN

A Jewish commencement speaker: "Today more than at any other time in history, humanity stands at the crossroads. One road leads to total despair. The other—to complete annihilation. Let us pray that we will have the wisdom to choose the right way."

WOODY ALLEN

May God bless and keep the Czar . . . far away from us!

FIDDLER ON THE ROOF

My parents worshipped Old World
values: God and carpeting.

WOODY ALLEN

In the old days, a man was known
by the company he kept. Nowadays,
he's known by the one he merges.

JACK BENNY

If you want to get on with the
Israelis, praise them. Tell them
openly to their faces that you think
they are wonderful. At first I thought
such statements might embarrass
them. But not at all. They can face
the truth. They say it themselves.

AUTHOR UNKNOWN

I'm Jewish with an explanation.

WOODY ALLEN

My grandfather was very depressed.
He used to drag a portable Wailing
Wall around the house.

RICHARD LEWIS, COMEDIAN

Zionism—One Jew talking another
Jew into moving to Israel on the
money of a third.

AUTHOR UNKNOWN

The whole of Holland is proof of
what man can create on the most
thankless soil.

THEODOR HERZL

We did not all come over on the
same ship, but we were all in the
same boat.

BERNARD M. BARUCH, AMERICAN BUSINESSMAN
AND STATESMAN

If my grandmother had four wheels,
she would be a baby carriage.

GOLDA MEIR

Spring ahead, fall back, winter in
Miami Beach.

AUTHOR UNKNOWN

Israel is the land of milk and honey.
Florida is the land of milk of
magnesia.

SAM LEVINSON, HUMORIST

"I'm going to Israel to see the
pyramids."

FRANK SINATRA, AT A FRIAR'S CLUB BANQUET,
A FEW DAYS AFTER THE SIX-DAY WAR

I'm just staying in America for one year.
EVERY ISRAELI IN AMERICA

Next year in Jerusalem. And if you should survive, then the following year take a nice cruise.
AUTHOR UNKNOWN

9
LOVE . . . AND/OR
MARRIAGE

Why did King Solomon have a
thousand wives? So when he came
home from work he'd at least find
one in a good mood.
>   ISAAC BASHEVIS SINGER

The world is built of love.
>   PSALMS 89:3

No man is happier than his wife.
>   AUTHOR UNKNOWN

Marriage is like a long banquet with the dessert served first.

NINETEENTH-CENTURY RUSSIAN-JEWISH PROVERB

Why do Jewish men die before their wives? Because they want to.

AUTHOR UNKNOWN

A man's mother might be his misfortune, but his wife is his own fault.

GROUCHO MARX

The holy spirit can rest only upon a married man, for an unmarried man is but half a man, and the holy spirit does not rest on what is imperfect.

AUTHOR UNKNOWN

He who does not marry is without true joy, without blessing, without happiness, without protection, without peace.

TALMUD, YEBEMOT 62

Never let the same dog bite you twice.

SOPHIE TUCKER, ON PHILANDERING HUSBANDS

No man who remains unmarried deserves the name of man.

TALMUD, YEBEMOT 63

If it is true that girls are inclined to marry men like their fathers, it is understandable why mothers cry at weddings.

GERTRUDE STEIN

Jewish men don't want wives—they want mothers.

SOPHIE TUCKER

Jewish women don't want husbands—they want wives.

MYRON COHEN

A man is forbidden to pluck out or dye even a single gray hair—unless this proves to be a handicap with regard to marriage or in obtaining a suitable job.

AUTHOR UNKNOWN

Hatred stirs up love, but love covers all transgressions.

PROVERBS 10:12

Loving you is like rising to the clouds in worlds reached only by imagination.

LADINO (SPANISH–JEWISH) LOVE SONG

Love is stronger than death, passion is unyielding as the grave; its flames are flames of fire. A flame of God.

SONG OF SONGS 8:6

It is impossible for man to live without woman, and it is impossible for woman to live without man, and it is impossible for both to live without the Divine Presence.

JERUSALEM TALMUD, BERAKHOT, 9:1

Love without jealousy is not true love.

THE ZOHAR

The day I married your mother I
could have eaten her alive. Now I
wish I had!

Mr. Ben Lipnick, Rego Park, New York

Grandchildren don't make a man
feel old; it's the knowledge that he's
married to a grandmother.

Overheard poolside, Fort Lauderdale,
Florida

Even a bad match can produce good
children.

Author unknown

Husband and wife are one flesh, but
have different wallets.

Mr. Sam Melnick, Melnick Dry Cleaning,
Syosset, New York

It is a dumb husband indeed who does not get the point when his wife starts wrapping his lunch in a road map.

SAM LEVINSON

When male turns his face from female, woe unto the world.

THE ZOHAR

If a married couple fights, they should reread their *ketubah* (wedding contract).

BAAL SHEM TOV

It is better to live in the desert than with a contentious, vexatious wife.

PROVERBS 21:19

A continual dripping on a rainy day
and a contentious woman are alike;
trying to restrain either is like
restraining the wind or grasping oil in
one's right hand.

PROVERBS 27:15–16

Rabbi Joshua bar Nachmani said:
"Premature aging is triggered by four
causes: fear, aggravation brought on
by one's children, an evil wife, and
war."

MIDRASH, TANCHUMA CHAYE SARAH 2

To a wedding you walk, to a divorce
you run.

HENNY YOUNGMAN

If you are angry with your mother-in-law, you yell at her daughter.

YIDDISH PROVERB

When a marriage ends, the altar sheds tears.

TALMUD

The rich widow's tears dry quickly.

HUNGARIAN–JEWISH PROVERB

10
MONEY

Money talks—it says goodbye.

GROUCHO MARX

A man sent a postcard from Las
Vegas to a friend: Having a
wonderful time. Wish I could afford
it.

MYRON COHEN

We were awfully poor. But we had
the things money can't buy—unpaid
bills.

BARBRA STREISAND

I wish my son would be less interested in writing about Capital and more interested in making some.

KARL MARX'S MOTHER

God loves the poor but helps the rich.

AUTHOR UNKNOWN

I've been poor and I've been rich. Rich is better.

SOPHIE TUCKER

Some people may be compared to new shoes: the cheaper they are the louder they squeak.

AUTHOR UNKNOWN

There are many who despise wealth, but few who are willing to part with it.

ECCLESIASTES 5

Do not show the depth of your heart, nor your wallet.

TALMUD, HAGIGAH 14

Rabbi Chayim of Sanz said, "The merit of charity is so great that I am happy to give to one hundred beggars even if only one might actually be needy. Some people, however, act as if they are exempt from giving to one hundred beggars in the event that one might be a fraud."

DARKAY CHAYIM (THE PATHS OF LIFE), sixteenth century

What good is money in the hand of a fool?

PROVERBS 17:16

Why do you spend money on that which is not bread?

AUTHOR UNKNOWN

Nobody is ever impoverished through the giving of charity.

MOSES MAIMONIDES

The heart grows hard quicker in riches than an egg in boiling water.

AUTHOR UNKNOWN

He who gives charity in secret is greater than Moses.

THE TALMUD

The lover of money is not satisfied
with money.

ECCLESIASTES 5:9

Whenever the Jews were barred
from a neighborhood, they pooled
their economic power and
purchased that neighborhood. If they
were banned from a hotel, they
bought the hotel.

MALCOLM X, *THE AUTOBIOGRAPHY OF
MALCOLM X*

Lend money and you acquire an
enemy.

ANCIENT HEBREW PROVERB

The rich will do everything for the
poor but get off their backs.

KARL MARX

A man should give no charity at all rather than give it publicly.

JUDAH BEN SAMUEL HA-HASID OF REGENSBERG, *SAFER HASIDISM* (twelfth century)

Money is the cause of good things to a good man and evil things to a bad man.

PHILO OF ALEXANDRIA, FIRST-CENTURY HELLENISTIC-JEWISH PHILOSOPHER

The Torah gives light, the Torah burns, but only the dollar gives warmth.

YIDDISH PROVERB

It is easier to make money than to keep it.

AUTHOR UNKNOWN

Poverty becomes a Jew like a red ribbon on a white horse.

AUTHOR UNKNOWN

The rich man has his brains in his wallet.

YIDDISH PROVERB

Better to die upright than to live on your knees.

HEBREW PROVERB

Three things cannot be hidden: love, coughing, and poverty.

HEBREW PROVERB

When people talk about a wealthy man of my creed, they call him an Israelite; but if he is poor, they call him a Jew.

HEINRICH HEINE

The three Jewish contact sports are chess, Monopoly, and small claims court.

MRS. RUTH GOLDSTEIN, DELROY BEACH, FLORIDA

More meat, more worms.

TALMUD, AVOT 2:7

Money buys everything except brains.

JACK E. LEONARD, COMEDIAN

The more flesh, the more worms;
the more property, the more anxiety;
the more wives, the more witchcraft;
the more maid-servants, the more
lewdness; the more men-servants,
the more robbery.

HILLEL, AVOT 2:8

11
SEX

Girls who start out playing with fire usually end up cooking over it.

MRS. ROSE NEEDLEBAUM, CENTURY VILLAGE, BOCA RATON, FLORIDA

When a man brings home flowers for his wife for no reason, it's a safe bet that there's a reason.

SOPHIE TUCKER

Marriage is a game of give and take. What you don't give, she takes.

HENNY YOUNGMAN

To us, the sexual act is worthy, good, and beneficial even to the soul. No other human activity compares with it, when performed with pure and clean intention it is certainly holy. . . . Health accrues to the body, too, when the act is performed in proper measure as to frequency and quality.

RABBI JACOB EMDEN, MEDIEVAL JEWISH SCHOLAR

A man is required to give his wife pleasure if she shows desire by her manner of dress or action.

BABYLONIAN TALMUD, PESACHIM 72B

If it wasn't for pickpockets, some men would have no sex lives at all.

RODNEY DANGERFIELD

Sex is the most wholesome,
beautiful, and sacred act that money
can buy.

JACK BENNY

A man's wife is permitted to him,
and, with her, he is allowed to do as
he pleases. He may cohabit with her
whenever he pleases, kiss her
whenever he pleases, and cohabit
naturally or unnaturally.

JACOB BEN ASHER, THIRTEENTH-CENTURY RABBI

A man who seeks only his sexual
satisfaction is "a thief who steals
away in the night."

TALMUD

Hands too can perform evil deeds and then they are ugly. So it is with the genitals.

NACHMANIDES, *IGGERET HA-KODES*
(translated by David Feldman)

Sexual intercourse is holy and pure when carried on properly, in the proper time, and with the proper intention. No one should claim that this is ugly or unseemly, God forbid.

NACHMANIDES, *IGGERET HA-KODES*
(translated by David Feldman)

Upon my bed at night I saw him whom my soul loves.

SONG OF SOLOMON 3:1

I sleep, but my heart wakes. Hark,
my beloved is knocking, saying,
open to me, my sister, my love, my
dove, my undefiled, for my head is
filled with dew, and my hair with the
drops of the night. I have put off my
coat, how shall I put it on?

SONG OF SONGS 5:2–3

All is credited to the woman.

MIDRASH, GENESIS RABBAH 17:12

To the extent that you are able,
avoid gazing upon women, even
upon their clothes.

SIXTEENTH-CENTURY CUSTOM, SAFED, ISRAEL

How graceful are your feet in sandals, O queenly maiden! Your rounded thighs are like jewels, the work of a master hand.

SONG OF SONGS 7:1

When a husband is in union with his wife, the Shechinah (divine presence) is with them.

NACHMANIDES

Three things are too wonderful for me, four I do not understand: the way of an eagle in the sky, the way of a serpent on a rock, the way of a ship on the high seas, and the way of a man with a young woman.

PROVERBS 30:18–19

Let him kiss me with the kisses of his mouth, for his love is better than wine.

SONG OF SONGS

How much better is thy love than wine, and the smell of thy ointments than all spices!

SONG OF SONGS, 4:10

A harlot is a deep pit; a forbidden woman is a narrow well. She too lies in wait as if for prey, and destroys the unfaithful among men.

PROVERBS 23:27–28

A man who loves wisdom brings joy to his father, but he who keeps company with prostitutes will lose his wealth.

PROVERBS 29:3

I will not punish your daughters when they play the harlot, nor your brides when they commit adultery; for the men themselves go aside with harlots, and sacrifice with cult prostitutes, and the people without understanding shall come to ruin.

HOSEA 4:14

If your evil inclination is strong, you are obliged to marry, because otherwise you might be afflicted with sexual thoughts.

MAIMONIDES, *A GUIDE FOR THE PERPLEXED*

Can a man rake embers into his breast without burning his clothes? Can a man walk on live coals without scorching his feet? It is the same for a man who sleeps with another man's wife—none who touches her will go unpunished.

PROVERBS 6:27–29

Seeing a married woman's hair is the equivalent of seeing her naked.

ORTHODOX JEWISH LAW

Such is the way of an adulteress: she eats, wipes her mouth, and says, "I have done no wrong." What a rare find is a capable wife! Her worth is far beyond that of rubies.

PROVERBS 31:10

Had we but world enough, and time,
this coyness Lady were no crime . . .
You should if you please refuse to
the conversion of the Jews.

ANDREW MARVELL, ENGLISH POET, TO HIS COY
MISTRESS

Man's eye, ear, and nose are not
under his direct control.

MIDRASH, B'REISHITH RABBAH 67

Man's eye is never satisfied.

PROVERBS 27

His left hand is under my head, and
his right hand embraces me.

SONG OF SONGS 8:3

Your rounded thighs are like jewels,
the work of the hands of an artist.
Your navel is like a round goblet,
that never lacks blended wine. Your
belly is like a heap of wheat set
about with lilies. Your two breasts
are like two fawns, the twins of a
gazelle. Your neck is like a tower of
ivory, your eyes like the pools in
Heshbon, by the gate of Bath-
rabbim. Your nose is like the tower
of the Lebanon, which looks toward
Damascus.

SONG OF SONGS 7:2–5

His left hand is under my head, and
his right hand embraces me.

SONG OF SONGS 8:3

My cousin was very successful, a lawyer. His wife got orgasm insurance. If he failed to satisfy her sexually, Mutual of Omaha had to pay her.

WOODY ALLEN

The only things I believe in are sex and death, two things that occur once in a lifetime. But at least after death, you're not nauseous.

WOODY ALLEN

12
TALK, TALK, TALK

I don't think I've ever met a quiet Jew.

PAUL MARTLAND, RIGHTEOUS GENTILE, OVERHEARD IN THE RASCAL HOUSE RESTAURANT, BOCA RATON, FLORIDA

He who praises himself shows that he is ignorant.

THE ZOHAR

What is the sign of a fool? He talks too much.

THE ZOHAR

A passerby who gets embroiled in someone else's quarrel is like one who seizes a dog by its ears.

PROVERBS 26:17

The Kutzkir Rebbe is the only one I've read about, and no one knows what to make of his spending the last twenty years of his life in silence . . . but being Jewish begins where words stop, where words can go no further.

JULIUS LESTER

One who unprotestingly listens to an evil tongue is morally of lower caliber than the one who possesses one. Were it not for those willing to listen, no damage could be caused.

AUTHOR UNKNOWN

A wise person does not shout and scream when speaking, but talks gently with all people and never raises his voice unduly.

MAIMONIDES, *MISHNAH TORAH*

He who disgraces his friend in the presence of others, it is as if he sheds blood.

TALMUD, BABA METZIA 58

Capitalism is like a dead herring in the moonlight—it shines, but it still stinks!

BILLY WILDER AND I.A.L. DIAMOND, FROM THE 1961 MOVIE *ONE, TWO, THREE*

You can tell an ass by his long ears—a fool by his long tongue.

AUTHOR UNKNOWN

Thou shalt not take up a false
report. (Don't spread gossip.)
ExODUS 23:1

Happiness is not having what you
want, but wanting what you have.
HYMAN JUDAH SCHACHTEL

As long as words are in your mouth,
you are their lord; the moment you
utter them, you are their slave.
IBN GABIROL, *CHOICE OF PEARLS*

If speech is worth one coin, silence
is worth two.
AUTHOR UNKNOWN

Words should be weighed, not
counted.
AUTHOR UNKNOWN

Death and life are in the power of
the tongue.

PROVERBS 18:21

The ancient Hebrews regarded the
history of the world as a great
lawsuit between themselves and the
heathens.

AUTHOR UNKNOWN

Walls have ears.

MIDRASH, TEHILLIM 7

Where there are two Jews, there are
three opinions.

ANCIENT HEBREW PROVERB

13
TALMUDIC PROVERBS

The Lord has given woman greater maturity of judgment than man.

TALMUD, NIDDAH 45B

The greater the man, the greater are his evil inclinations.

TALMUD, SUKKAH 52

An ignorant man will always be the first to be heard.

TALMUD, MAGILLAH 12

A foolish saint is a supposedly pious
man who sees a woman drowning
but does not want to rescue her
because she is unclothed.

TALMUD, SOTAH 21B

Rabbi Ben Azzai had no children and
was criticized by his colleagues for
this. He responded, "What can I do?
My soul is in love with the Torah.
The world will have to be populated
by others."

AUTHOR UNKNOWN

He who says, "I will sin and then
repent, I will sin and then repent, I
will sin and then repent," will be
given no opportunity to repent.

TALMUD, YOMA 85B

It is written in the Torah, "You shall
not imprint any marks upon you"
(Leviticus 19:28). The prohibition
applies to a mark which is etched
into the skin so that it can never be
erased. That is, tattooing is
forbidden.

CODE OF JEWISH LAW

Tats rule.

JOSH BEIGELMAN, JOSH'S TAT PARLOR, VENICE
BEACH, CALIFORNIA

The desire to sin is at first like a
passerby, then like a lodger, and
finally like the master of the house.

THE TALMUD

Three things to which the Torah is
compared: to the desert, to fire, and
to water. This is to tell you that just
as these three things are free to all
who come into the world, so also are
the words of the Torah, free to all
who come into the world.

MIDRASH, MEKHILTA

Sleep is a sixtieth part of death.

THE TALMUD

Flight (running away from responsibilities)
goes before a fall.

TALMUD, SOTAH 8:6

It's better to be a tail to lions than a
head to foxes.

RABBI MATTITHYA ARUT, 4:20

A gentile came before Rabbi Hillel and asked to be converted on the condition that Hillel teach him the entire Torah while standing on one foot. Hillel said to him, "What is hateful to you, to your fellow man, don't do. That's the entirety of the Torah; everything else is elaboration. So go and study."

TALMUD, SHABBAT 31A

There is time enough for worry when the worry comes.

TALMUD, BERACHOT 9

Do not do unto your neighbor that which is disagreeable to you.

TALMUD, SHABBAT 31

To study without review is like
sowing without reaping.

AUTHOR UNKNOWN

People stab each other with their
tongues.

TALMUD, YOMA 9

A man is known by his laughter.

TALMUD, ERUVIN 65B

One human life outweighs all
creation.

THE TALMUD

If one saves a life, it is as if one
saves a whole world.

TALMUD, SANHEDRIN

The right of the working man always
has precedence.

TALMUD, BABA METZIA 77

A person should always go up in
holiness and not go down.

TALMUD, SABBATH 21B

It matters not whether one does
much or little, if only he directs his
heart to heaven.

TALMUD, BERACHOT, 17A

To extend hospitality is loftier than
to greet the Divine Presence.

TALMUD, TRACTATE SHABBOS

14
UNTIL DEATH . . .

For their twentieth wedding
anniversary, Shimsky bought his wife
a cemetery plot. As their twenty-first
anniversary approached, Mrs.
Shimsky asked "What are you going
to give this year for our
anniversary?"

"Nothing," he replied. "You still
didn't use what I gave you last year."

ESTHER FUCHS, *HUMOR AND SEXISM*

For the ignorant, old age is a winter
time; for the wise, harvest time.

TALMUD, HAGIGAH 14

Item from the reading of a Jewish
will by the lawyer to the relatives:
"And to my cousin Louie, who I said
I would remember in my will—'Hello,
Louie!'"

CHRISTIE DAVIES, *JEWISH JOKES, ANTI-SEMITIC JOKES, AND HEBREDNIAN JOKES*

Some are old in their youth, others
young in their old age.

AUTHOR UNKNOWN

With the aged is wisdom, and with
length of days comes understanding.

JOB 12:12

Charity saves a person from death.

AUTHOR UNKNOWN

Trust not in yourself until the day of your death.

HILLEL, AVOT, 2:5

A baby enters the world with closed hands. A person leaves the world with open hands. The first says, "The world is mine." The second says, "I can take nothing with me."

MIDRASH, ECCLESIASTES RABBAH

As he came out of his mother's womb, so must he depart at last, naked as he came. He can take nothing of his work to carry with him. So what is the good of his toiling for the wind? Besides, all his days, he eats in darkness with much vexation and grief and anger.

ECCLESIASTES 5:15–16

What profit has man of all his work
with which he wearies himself under
the sun? One generation passes
away and another comes; the earth
alone abides forever.

ECCLESIASTES

Grief breaks the body.

TALMUD, BERACHOT 58

Allen: What are you doing Saturday
night?
Girl: Committing suicide.
Allen: How about Friday night?

WOODY ALLEN, *PLAY IT AGAIN, SAM*

Death is nature's way of telling you
to slow down.

WOODY ALLEN

Shrouds have no pockets.

HEBREW PROVERB

Death is a night between two days.

RABBI MAURICE LAMM, *THE JEWISH WAY OF DEATH AND MOURNING*

He who fears death is really afraid of life.

DAVID WEINBERG

15
WISDOM AND
FOOLISHNESS

An empty-headed man will become
intelligent when an ass's colt is born
a man.

JOB 11:12

Better is a lowly and wise child than
an old and foolish king.

ECCLESIASTES 4:13

Better to lose with a wise man than
to win with a fool

PROVERBS 29

Why did God create goyim? In His wisdom, he knew *somebody* had to buy retail.

MR. JONATHAN FINK, FINK BROTHERS, INC., ROSLYN, NEW YORK

A man can secure knowledge only by sacrifice.

TALMUD, GITTIN 56

Much study is a wearying of the flesh.

ECCLESIASTES 12:12

Wine is a scoffer, strong drink a brawler, he who is muddled by them will not grow wise.

PROVERBS 20:1

The wise man's mind is on the house of mourning, but the fool's mind is on the house of rejoicing.

ECCLESIASTES 7:4

He who will not seek knowledge, knowledge certainly will not seek him.

MIDRASH, PROVERBS 2

The fool thinks that all people are fools.

MIDRASH, KOHELET RABBAH 86

He who has much knowledge suffers much pain.

ECCLESIASTES 1

Do not be overly righteous and do not be too terribly wise. Why should you cause yourself trouble? Do not be overly wicked and do not be a fool. Why should you die when your time has not come?

ECCLESIASTES 7:16–17

Wisdom is a tree of life to those who grasp her, and whoever holds on to her is happy.

PROVERBS 3:18

A rebuke works on an intelligent man more than one hundred blows on a fool.

PROVERBS 17:10

It is better to meet a bereaved she-bear than a fool with his nonsense.

PROVERBS 17:12

Who is wise? He who learns from all men. Who is mighty? He who subdues his nature. Who is rich? He who is happy with his lot. Who is worthy of honor? He who respects his fellow men.

BEN ZOMA, AVOT 4:1

A wise man understands his own foolishness.

HEBREW PROVERB

I found that wisdom is superior to folly as light is superior to darkness; a wise man has his eyes in his head, whereas a fool walks in darkness. But I also realized that the same fate awaits them both...Alas, the wise man dies, just like the fool!

ECCLESIASTES 2:13–16

The attempt to combine wisdom and power has only rarely been successful, and then only for a short while.

ALBERT EINSTEIN

The tree of learning bears the noblest fruit.

AUTHOR UNKNOWN

Truth is its own witness.

AUTHOR UNKNOWN

For a wise man, a gentle hint; for a fool, a fist.

MIDRASH, PROVERBS 22

A poor man's wisdom is scorned, and his words are not heeded.

ECCLESIASTES 15:9

16
WORK

If my theory of relativity is proven successful, Germany will claim me as a German and France will declare that I am a citizen of the world. Should they prove my theory untrue, France will say that I am a German and Germany will declare that I am a Jew.

ALBERT EINSTEIN

History is the study of other people's mistakes.

PHILIP GUEDELLA, ESSAYIST AND HISTORIAN

If one has no means of livelihood,
he is free to die of hunger.

SHALOM ALEICHEM

To succeed in business, always
follow two principles: honesty and
wisdom. Honesty means that if you
promise to deliver a shipment of
goods on the twenty-fourth of March,
you deliver the shipment. Wisdom
means being smart enough not to
promise anything.

SAM LEVINSON

He who will not work, will not eat.
He who tends the fig tree shall eat
its fruits.

PROVERBS 27

You can learn seven things from a thief. One, he goes about his business at night. Two, if one night doesn't work, he tries another. Three, he and his partners are friends with each other. Four, he risks his life for a trifle. Five, what he takes he sells at a small profit. Six, he is patient of misfortunes. Seven, he esteems his profession above all others.

RABBI DOV BAER OF MEZHIRECH, THE GREAT MAGGID

One thing acquired through pain is better for man than one hundred things easily achieved.

MIDRASH

In winter the lazy man does not plow; at harvest time he seeks, and finds nothing.

PROVERBS 20:4

Let not a man say, "I come from a noble and distinguished family and I cannot stoop to work and degrade myself." Fool, your creator, God himself, performed work before you were born!

MIDRASH N'ELAM, VENICE EDITION (1663)

Labor is a craft, but perfect rest is an art.

ABRAHAM JOSHUA HESCHEL

17
YIDDISH PROVERBS

Yiddish is the mother language of Eastern European Jews. Hebrew was called *loshon kodesh*—the holy tongue, suitable only for prayer or religious study, too important and proper to speak in the street. Yiddish, on the other hand, was the people's language—a way to express feelings, vent anger, escape oppression, fall in and out of love. Yiddish borrows (read: steals) words from every language where Jews lived: German, Russian, Hebrew, English, even fossilized bits of Latin found their way into the *mama loshon*, the Yiddish way of saying "mother tongue."

Yiddish just plain sounds funny. All those guttural sounds, improbable

combinations of consonants, and hysterically funny words make the language the perfect vehicle for expressing the truth—sometimes bitter, sometimes caustic, and sometimes even wildly optimistic—of the day-to-day struggles with life. *Verklempt, fablunged, farbissene, ungepatchke*—no other language can possibly claim words like that. And how can you not take such words and come up with funny, insightful, and honest statements about life?

When I was a little boy, Yiddish was a source of massive frustration for me. My mother and her parents, whenever they wanted to speak in front of me without my understanding, would turn to Yiddish. I resolved that one day I'd understand the language myself. To my regret, I've never truly mastered it. But the most surprising aspect of my Yiddish education was the relative lack of Yiddish curses and insults. I thought that Yiddish would be full of that stuff ("May you grow like an

eggplant—straight into the ground"). While Yiddish does offer some really nasty zingers, for the most part the Yiddish proverbs I found to share with you are rather upbeat.

This is a credit to the basic Jewish personality. Even when things were darkest—and for centuries life in Eastern Europe for Jews was no picnic—we never lost our basic optimism and faith in the future. As the early pioneers of the State of Israel sang, things will get better, "if not tomorrow, then the next day." That optimism in the face of relentless pressure is what being Jewish is all about. For your consideration: a collection of Yiddish one-liners, honed in the crucible of Eastern European Jewish life.

Enjoy!

If you can't say something nice, say it in Yiddish.

MOLLY PICON

To err is human, to forgive is unthinkable.

YIDDISH PROVERB

All your hair should fall out except for one—and it should have dandruff.

YIDDISH CURSE

You should own a hotel with one thousand rooms and have a bellyache in each one!

YIDDISH CURSE

May all the sewers on Ocean
Parkway back up in your breakfast.

YIDDISH CURSE

Better a crooked foot than a crooked
mind.

YIDDISH PROVERB

An ounce of luck is worth more than
a pound of gold.

YIDDISH PROVERB

A slap from a wise man is better
than a kiss from a fool.

YIDDISH PROVERB

Women eat you up when you're dead and worries eat you up while you're alive.

Yiddish proverb

What a fool can undo, ten wise men cannot fix.

Yiddish proverb

Always whisper the names of diseases.

Yiddish proverb

You can't ride two horses with one *tuchas.*

Yiddish proverb

With one *tuchas*, you cannot dance at two weddings.

YIDDISH PROVERB

To get old is to forget everything but your resentments.

THIS PROVERB IS ALSO ATTRIBUTED TO THE IRISH, BUT WE HAD IT FIRST.

A half-truth is a whole lie.

YIDDISH PROVERB

A bad conscience is a snake in one's heart.

YIDDISH PROVERB

If a Jew breaks a leg, he thanks God
he did not break both legs; if he
breaks both, he thanks God he did
not break his neck.

YIDDISH PROVERB

One mitzvah can change the world.
Two will just make you feel tired.

YIDDISH PROVERB

Life is like a child's undershirt—short
and soiled.

YIDDISH PROVERB

Where people love you, go rarely;
where you are hated, go not at all.

YIDDISH PROVERB

The ugliest life is better than the nicest death.

YIDDISH PROVERB

It is written: Silence is wisdom.

YIDDISH PROVERB

The longest road in the world is the one that leads from your pocket.

YIDDISH PROVERB

You dig your grave with your teeth.

YIDDISH PROVERB

Love is sweet, but it's nice to have bread with it.

YIDDISH PROVERB

The man who marries for money earns it.

YIDDISH PROVERB

De calla es tzu schin (The bride is too pretty so watch out!)

IRVING ROZEN, MY GRANDFATHER

God punishes with one hand and blesses with the other.

YIDDISH PROVERB

A good kugel will sink in mercury.

YIDDISH PROVERB

From snow you can't make a cheesecake.

YIDDISH PROVERB

The rich man should eat when he
has an appetite, and the poor man
when he has food.

YIDDISH PROVERB

It's much better to be dead drunk
than dead hungry.

YIDDISH PROVERB

18
What Is Enough? Too Much: Wisdom From the Lower East Side

The Lower East Side of Manhattan in New York City is fondly remembered as the first home in the New World for millions of immigrant Jews—unless you actually lived there, in which case your memories may be anything but fond.

Backyard outhouses, little privacy, nonexistent heat and hot water, crowded tenements—all of this must have come as a rude shock to the hundreds of thousands of Eastern European Jews who'd been told that America's streets were paved with gold.

The goal of practically every Jew (not to mention every other ethnic group) living on the Lower East Side was to get out as quickly as possible—to move uptown to Washington Heights or to the Bronx, to Brooklyn (which may have been America's first suburbia), or to anywhere but those teeming, dangerous streets.

And yet. From hardship comes wisdom, and with wisdom, in many cases, comes humor. Herewith, some pearls of wishes from the Lower East Side. The sources of these gems are unknown, handed down as they were by the denizens of streets with names like Delancey, Grand, Essex, Hester, and Houston (pronounced HOW-ston).

What is love? Love is a potato. It's got eyes, but it's blind.

Why are you only deaf? Why aren't you also dumb?

When you see two cows lying in a field, one of them is a bull.

Never double-cross me behind my back.

Always do one thing and do it right. But have a few things on the side, too.

To my late mother-in-law: May she rest where she is.

What is a wife but a needle shower? Everywhere you turn, she sticks you.

Life is like a seesaw: today you're poor, tomorrow you're poorer.

What are clothes but freckles? They cover you up, but they don't meaning nothing.

The Lower East Side is the only place where clothes don't make the man. They can't afford them.

What is enough? Too much.

What is life? Like playing cards with two decks, it works fine.

Having a lot of business is like having a lot of teeth—they can all go bad.

Anything worth saying is worth repeating a thousand times.

May God protect you from *goyishe* hands and from Yiddish tongues.

If you're going to do something wrong, enjoy it.

Hope for miracles but don't rely on one.

Bibliography

Allen, Woody, *Getting Even*, New York: Random House, 1971.

Allen, Woody, *Play It Again Sam*, New York: Random House, 1969.

Appel, Gersion, *The Concise Code of Jewish Law*, New York: Ktav Publishing House, 1977.

Asubel, Nathan, ed., *A Treasury of Jewish Humor*, New York: M Evans and Company, 1988.

Axelrad, Albert S., *Meditations of a Maverick Rabbi*, Chappaqua, NY: Rossel Books, 1985.

Baron, Joseph L., *A Treasury of Jewish Quotations*, New York: Crown Publishers, 1956.

Ben Zion, Raphael, trans., *An Anthology of Jewish Mysticism*, New York: Judaica Press, 1981.

Bernstein, Ellen, ed., *Ecology and the Jewish Spirit*, Woodstock, Vermont: Jewish Lights Publishing, 1998.

Bialik, Hayam Nahman and Ravnitzky, *Yenoshua Hana, The Book of Legends*, trans. by William G. Braude, New York: Schocken Books, 1992.

Birnbaum, Phillip, ed., *Maimonides' Mishna Torah*, New York: Hebrew Publishing Company, 1967.

Block, Abraham P., *Midrashic Comments on the Torah for Sabbaths and Festivals*, Hoboken, New Jersey: Ktav Publishing House, 1991.

Bokser, Ben Zion, *The Wisdom of the Talmud*, New York: Philosophical Library, 1951.

Braude, William G., and Kapstein, Israel J., trans., *Tanna Debe Eliyyahu: The Lore of the School of Elijah*, Philadelphia: Jewish Publication Society of America, 1981.

Brayer, Menachem M., *The Jewish Woman in Rabbinic Literature*, Hoboken, New Jersey: Ktav Publishing House, 1986.

Schulweis, Harold M., *For Those Who Can't Believe*, New York: HarperCollins, 1994.

Cohen, John, ed., *The Essential Lenny Bruce*, New York: Ballantine Books, 1967.

Cohen, Myron, *The Myron Cohen Joke Book*, New York: Gramercy Publishing Company, 1978.

Cowan, Lore, and Maurice, *The Wit of the Jews*, London, England: Aurora Publishers, 1970.

Dabidoff, Henry, *A World Treasury of Proverbs*, New York: Random House, 1946.

Diamant, Anita, and Cooper, Howard, *Living a Jewish Life*, New York: Harper Perennial, 1991.

Donin, Hayim, *Halevy*, New York: Basic Books, 1972.

Dressner, Samuel H., ed., *I Asked for Wonder*—A Spiritual Anthology—Abraham Joshua Heschel, New York: Crossroad Press, 1983.

Eilbirt, Henry, *What Is a Jewish Joke?* Northvale, New Jersey: Jason Aronson, 1991.

Eisen, Arnold M., *The Chosen People in America*, Bloomington, Indiana: Indiana University Press, 1983.

Fendel, Zechariah, *Anvil of Sinai*, New York: Hashkafah Publications, 1977.

Freeman, Gordon M., *The Heavenly Kingdom: Aspects of Political Thought in the Talmud and Midrash*, Lanham, Maryland: The Jerusalem Center for Public Affairs, 1986.

Fuchs, Yitzchak Yaacov, *Halichos bas Yisrael: A Woman's Guide to Jewish Observance*, Oak Park, Michigan: Targum Press, 1985.

Gold, Michael, *Jewish Folklore and Legend*, London, England: Hamlin Publishing Group, 1980.

Good, Edwin M., *Irony in the Old Testament*, Sheffield, England: The Almond Press, 1981.

Goodman, Phillip, *The Yom Kippur Anthology*, Philadelphia: The Jewish Publication Society of America, 1971.

Gordis, Robert, *Love and Sex, A Modern Jewish Perspective*, New York: Hippocrene Books, 1988.

Greenberg, Sidney, ed., *A Treasury of Comfort*, Hollywood, California: Wilshire Book Company, 1967.

Gross, David C., and Gross, Esther R., *Under the Wedding Canopy, Love and Marriage in Judaism*, New York: Hippocrene Books, 1996.

Guttmacher, Adolf, *Optimism and Pessimism in the Old and New Testaments*, Baltimore, Maryland: Friedenwald Company, 1903.

Hausdorff, David M., *A Book of Jewish Curiosities*, New York: Crown Publishers, 1955.

Heilman, Samuel, *Defenders of the Faith*, New York: Schocken Books, 1992.

Hertz, Joseph H., *Sayings of the Fathers*, New York: Berhman House, 1945.

Heschel, Abraham Joshua, *God In Search of Man*, Northvale, New Jersey: Jason Aronson, 1987.

———, *The Sabbath*, New York: Farrar, Straus, and Giroux, 1975.

Horowitz, Aron, *You Can Be Your Own Rabbi Most of the Time*, Toronto: Aron Horowitz Publications, 1985.

Jacobs, Louis, *What Does Judaism Say About...?*, New York: Quadrangle/New York Times Books, 1973.

Jung, Leo, ed., *The Jewish Library*, New York: McMillan, 1928.

Kagos, Fred, *1001 Yiddish Proverbs*, New York: Citadel Press, 1995.

Kaplan, Aryeh, *The Handbook of Jewish Thought*, New York: Mazniam Publishing Corp., 1979.

Kogel, Rene, and Katz, Zev, *Judaism in a Secular Age*, Hoboken, New Jersey: Ktav Publishing House, 1995.

Koltun, Liz, *The Jewish Woman—An Anthology*, Waltham, Massachusetts: Response, 1973.

Kushner, Lawrence, *The River of Light*, Chappaqua, New York: Rossel Books, 1981.

Lamm, Maurice, *The Jewish Way in Death and Mourning*, New York: Jonathan David, 1969.

Learsi, Rufus, *The River of Light*, Chappaqua, New York: Rossel Books, 1981.

Lester, Julius, *Lovsong—Becoming a Jew*, New York: Henry Holt and Co., 1988.

Lipman, Steve, *Laughter in Hell, The Use of Humor During the Holocaust*, Northvale, New Jersey: Jason Aronson, 1991.

Luzzatto, Moshe Chaim, *The Way of God*, trans. by Aryeh Kaplan, New York: Feldheim Publishers, 1977.

Martin Buber's Ten Rungs, New York: Citadel Press, 1995.

Mintz, Jerome R., *Legends of the Hasidim*, Chicago: University of Chicago Press.

Neuberger, Julia, *On Being Jewish*, London, England: Heinemann, 1995.

Neusner, Jacob, *Judaism's Theological Voice—The Melody of the Talmud*, Chicago: University of Chicago Press, 1995.

Newman, Lewis I., *The Hasidic Anthology*, Northvale, New Jersey: Jason Aronson, 1963.

Olsvanger, Immanuel, *L'chayim!*, New York: Schocken Books, 1941.

Otwell, John H., *And Sarah Laughed*, Philadelphia: The Westminster Press, 1977.

Peters, Madison C., ed., *Wit and Wisdom of the Talmud*, Folcroft Library, Editions 1980.

Reik, Theodor, *Jewish Wit*, New York: Gamut Press, 1962.

Riley, Dorothy Winbush, ed., *My Soul Looks Back 'Less I Forget,*

A Collection of Quotations by People of Color, New York: HarperCollins, 1993.

Rose, Aubrey, ed., *Judaism and Ecology*, London, England: Cassell Publishers, 1992.

Rosten, Leo, *Leo Rosten's Treasury of Jewish Quotations*, New York: McGraw Hill, 1972.

Rosten, Leo, *Hooray for Yiddish!*, New York: Simon & Schuster, 1982.

Schwartz, Howard, *The Captive Soul Over the Messiah*, New York: Schocken Books, 1983.

Seldes, George, *The Great Quotations*, New York: Lyle Stuart, 1960.

Silver, Abba Hillel, *Where Judaism Differed*, Philadelphia: Jewish Publication Society, 1957.

Spalding, Henry D., ed., *Encyclopedia of Jewish Humor*, New York: Jonathan David Publishers, 1969.

Tanakh, A New Translation of the Holy Scriptures, Philadelphia: The Jewish Publication Society, 1985.

The Eternal Light, New York: Harper and Row, 1966.

The Oxford Dictionary of Quotations, London, England: Oxford University Press, 1941.

Titelbaum, Elsa, *An Anthology of Jewish Humor and Maxims*, New York: Pardes Publishing House.

Townsend, John T., *Midrash Tanhuma*, Hoboken, New Jersey: Ktav Publishing House, 1989.

Treasury of Jewish Love, New York: Hippocrene Books, 1995.

Trepp, Leo, *The Complete Book of Jewish Obsevance*, New York: Behrman House, and Summit Books, 1980.

Visotsky, Burton L., trans., *The Midrash and Proverbs*, New Havaen: Yale University Press, 1992.

Wechsler, Harlan J., *What's So Bad About Guilt?*, New York: Simon & Schuster, 1990.

Weinberg, Rabbi Moishe, *Jewish Outreach: Halakahic Perspectives*, Hoboken, New Jersey: Ktav Publishing House, 1990.

Wolpe, David J., *In Speech and In Silence*, New York: Henry Holt, 1992.

Youngman, Henny, *Four Hundred Traveling Salesman's Jokes*, New York: Citadel Press, 1966.

Zevin, Shlomo Yosef, *A Treasury of Hasidic Tales on the Torah*, New York: Mesorah Publications, 1980.

Ziv, Avner, ed., *Jewish Humor*, Tel Aviv: Papyrus Publishing House, 1986.